A Family of Collectors

by Joanna Korba

illustrated by Bradley Clark

Scott Foresman
is an imprint of

Glenview, Illinois • Boston, Massachusetts • Chandler, Arizona
Upper Saddle River, New Jersey

Illustrations by Bradley Clark

ISBN 13: 978-0-328-51377-2
ISBN 10:   0-328-51377-6

4 5 6 7 8 9 10 V0FL 13 12 11

Chapter One

My mother collects English teacups and saucers. She displays them all over our dining room and living room. Each cup has its own holder, with a matching saucer propped up behind it. My mother never allows anyone to drink out of the cups.

When I ask her about this, she always says the same thing: "They are just for show, Tina."

"But what's the point of having them if you don't use them?" I asked her one day.

"Well, some of them are very valuable, of course . . ." she began.

"Oh, I get it!" I rushed in eagerly. "You're buying them to sell for money!"

"No, no, no," my mom said firmly. "I collect them because I like to look at them. Don't you think they're beautiful?" she asked. "Look at this one, Tina."

She reached for a nearby teacup. It was white, with a gold rim, and had flowers painted on it.

"See how shiny it is?" she said proudly. "And see how it looks as if it's glowing, like there is light inside it? That's because it's made of bone china."

Bone china or not, I still couldn't understand why Mom loved these cups so much, but I kept that to myself as I tried to learn more.

"That cup is made of bones from China?" I asked. "I thought you collected English teacups and saucers."

"I do," Mom said, as she put down the cup. "Let me explain."

"China is another name for porcelain," she said. "Porcelain was first made in China, hundreds of years ago. That's why people often call it china. For a long time the Chinese guarded the secret of how porcelain is made, but after a while their secret began to spread to other countries. Then, about two hundred years ago, the English added ash, made from animal bones, to make a special kind of porcelain called bone china. That's what I collect, English bone china."

As you can tell, my mom is full of information about teacups and saucers.

"Yes, I see," I answered politely. I felt that I should say something nice. "I like the gold around the top. It's pretty."

"Isn't it?" Mom asked eagerly. "I adore the ones that have gold rims. They are my favorites. I'm so glad that you like them too, Tina!"

As I left, my mom was turning the teacup around and around in the sunlight, staring at it. She had a dreamy smile on her face. I felt a bit guilty, pretending to like the cups, since I was really just trying to be polite.

I could tell that Mom wanted me to appreciate her love of collecting teacups and saucers, but the truth was, I still didn't get it.

Chapter Two

One night, not long after Mom showed me her teacups, there was a knock at my door. It was Dad. He closed the door behind him and said, "It's your mother's birthday in a couple of weeks. I think we should get her something special, and I know just the thing!"

"Great!" I said. I was glad to hear that Dad had already picked something out since I had not thought of any ideas for Mom's birthday gift. That would make things easy for me. I could just give him some of my allowance to pay for part of it and then help him wrap it up nicely. "What are we giving her?"

"A teacup and saucer to add to her collection," said Dad. "We can get her one at the All-State Collectibles Fair next weekend."

"But her collection is already so big!" I said, frowning. "Doesn't she have enough?"

Dad laughed. "A collector is never done collecting. We just have to make sure not to give Mom a teacup that she already has. I took some photos of her collection so we'll know which ones not to buy."

"Wow, Dad! You thought of everything," I said. "Whenever you want to go to the fair next weekend, I'll be ready."

"Excellent," my father said. "All-State Fair, here we come!"

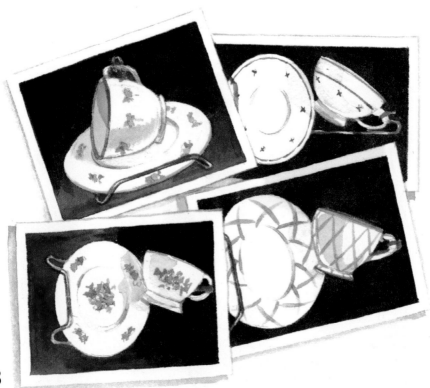

9

Chapter Three

The All-State Collectibles Fair comes to town only once a year, during a weekend in summer. Sellers come from all over the state with things that people collect, and each seller gets a certain area to display things.

People interested in buying collectibles pay seven dollars to go into the fair. Once they have paid, they can look at anything that is on display and for sale.

There are many different types of collectibles, which are sold at many different prices. You can find furniture, clothing, toys, books, artwork, tools, postcards, and anything else that people might collect. Some collectibles cost thousands of dollars, and others cost less than a dollar. At the All-State Collectibles Fair, there's something for everyone.

My father and I arrived at the fair at ten o'clock in the morning because we wanted to make sure we had plenty of time to look around. There were already many people wandering through the fair.

"This fair is enormous! Where should we start?" I asked.

"Most sellers specialize," Dad explained. "We need to find out which ones sell china. I'll check at the information desk. You wait here for me."

While I waited, I looked around at everyone else at the fair. Were all these people collectors like my mom? Did they keep buying more and more of the same thing too? I wished I could understand it all, but I couldn't. I felt like I was on a different planet.

Dad came back waving a map. "The woman at the information desk marked the best places to check for teacups and saucers," he said. Then Dad pointed to the right. "If we head down this way a bit, we'll come to one of the places."

As we walked along, he told me what we should look for.

"We want to get Mom a teacup and saucer that are in good shape," he said. "But remember, we're only interested in English bone china. Also, we need to look for a pattern that Mom doesn't have."

The first place we checked didn't have many nice cups and saucers. It didn't take us long to realize that we wouldn't find anything for Mom there, so we moved on.

The next place had many more to choose from. One of the cups had a gold rim and a pretty pattern, but when I turned it over, I noticed that the bottom was chipped. Then I saw the price. It was much too high for a chipped cup. I checked another item, but it was overpriced too.

I pulled my dad aside. "I don't think these prices are fair. They seem much too high to me."

My dad agreed. "They're too high," he whispered, "but I bet the next place will have better prices."

He was right. The next place had very good prices. We found a pretty cup and saucer that were both in good shape, and they were decorated with gold rims. But when Dad turned the cup over he shook his head.

"It's made in France, not England," he said. "And I think this pattern is very similar to one your mom already has." He checked the photos, pulled one out, and pointed. "See? It's almost the same. Let's head this way and keep looking."

Chapter Four

Dad and I walked along past more booths. As we neared the next place that sold china, I heard someone say, "Oh! That's so amazing!" I turned and saw a woman who was looking through a banged-up tube. Then she took the tube from her eye and looked it over. "I would buy it if it weren't in such bad shape," she said. The woman put the tube down on the table and walked away.

"What was that woman looking through?" I asked Dad. We both walked over to the table.

"It's a kaleidoscope," he said. Dad picked it up and looked through it. "What a great view!" he exclaimed.

"Hey, can I check it out?" I asked, reaching for it.

"Here you go," Dad said, handing it to me. "Hold it up to the light and look through it. As you look, turn this end."

There were all kinds of lights, patterns, and colors on display inside the tube. I saw images that were as beautiful as the feathers on a peacock and as colorful as a rainbow. Patterns of shapes and colors kept changing before my eyes, and lights flashed as each pattern changed. I couldn't put the kaleidoscope down!

I was still looking through it when I heard my dad's excited voice. "Tina, come and look at these cups!"

I was afraid to leave the kaleidoscope behind since there was the chance that someone would buy it. But the man at the table told me not to worry. "I can tell you love it. Shall I put it aside for you while you decide? That way, no one else can buy it in the meantime."

I trusted the man and handed the kaleidoscope back to him with a nod. Then I went over to my dad, who was holding a teacup in each hand.

"Both these cups are right for Mom," he said. "I just can't decide which one to pick."

"I like this one better," I decided, holding one up to my dad. "The colors are prettier."

"All right! We'll get it," my dad agreed. "Then maybe we'll look for a nice kaleidoscope for you."

"Really?" I grinned, but then I frowned. "What was wrong with the kaleidoscope I was looking at?" I asked.

"Well, it's kind of banged up, honey," my dad replied. "I'm sure we can find you a nicer one."

With Mom's gift taken care of, Dad and I began looking for kaleidoscopes. We saw plenty that were nice, but none created the beautiful images like the first one I'd seen.

We kept looking. Then I saw a boy carrying a kaleidoscope he'd just bought. I asked to look at it. It was nice on the outside, and I liked the patterns it made inside. He pointed us toward the booth where he'd bought it. We arrived at the booth only to be told by the woman running it that there were no kaleidoscopes left.

It was getting late in the day, and I didn't have any more energy to look for kaleidoscopes. Finally I said to my dad, "The first one was the best. I don't care if it's banged up on the outside. It's really beautiful inside, and I love it. It's definitely the one that I want."

As we made our way back to the first kaleidoscope booth, I began to get nervous. What if the man had decided that we weren't coming back? What if he had sold it while we were looking for Mom's present?

But my kaleidoscope was still there, safe and sound. "Hello!" the man called out cheerfully. "I knew you'd be back. I could see how much you loved this little kaleidoscope!"

"My dad's going to buy it for my birthday!" I told him. I couldn't stop smiling. "May I look at it again, before you wrap it up?"

The man handed the banged-up tube to me, and I held it up to the light and looked through. It was so beautiful! I hated to give it back to the man, even though I knew he would be wrapping it up especially for me.

I felt tired but very excited as Dad and I drove home from the fair. I couldn't wait to start using my new kaleidoscope!

Chapter Five

Mom had been busy all day, which was why she couldn't come to the fair with Dad and me. When we got back, she could tell we had been up to something. "What have you two been doing?" she asked suspiciously.

Dad and I did our best to keep our secret. "We haven't been up to anything," we said at the same time.

The morning of my mom's birthday, we placed her gift on the counter so she'd see it as soon as she walked into the kitchen. I'd carefully wrapped the cup and saucer in birthday paper and tied it with a bright ribbon.

Mom opened her birthday present before breakfast, and when she saw what was inside, she clapped her hands with joy.

"Why, these are beautiful!" she exclaimed, gently pulling the cup and saucer from their wrappings. "What a lovely pattern, and with a gold rim! How did you know that I'm fond of the gold rimmed cups?" she asked with a smile.

"I remembered what you said," I explained happily. "But it was Dad's idea to get you a teacup and saucer." I wanted to be honest and not take all the credit. "He even took pictures of your collection so we could give you one that's different from the others."

"Well then, you both deserve hugs," she said, as she came and hugged us both. Dad and I smiled at each other. We knew we had done well with Mom's birthday surprise!

A little while later, Mom motioned me over to the window. She was sitting there looking at her birthday present. That dreamy smile of hers, the one I had seen the last time we were looking at her teacups and saucers, was back again. "Look, Tina," she said.

"It's shiny and it glows," I said. "Am I right?"

"Right," my mom agreed happily. "I think you're starting to understand why I love to collect teacups and saucers."

"Definitely," I replied. "Especially because I'm now collecting beautiful things myself."

"Oh really?" Mom asked, with a curious expression on her face. "Like what?"

I turned to Dad. "Dad, is it OK to show Mom the present you got me at the fair?"

"Sure. Why not?"

Dad brought out my present. I unwrapped the kaleidoscope and handed it to Mom.

"It's worn on the outside," I told her, "but look inside."

"Oh, how beautiful!" Mom gasped, as she looked through it. She handed it back to me.

I held my kaleidoscope up to the light and looked inside. I felt a dreamy smile spreading across my face, a smile just like the ones on Mom's face when she looks at her teacups!

Toy Collectors

People of all ages like to collect toys. Toy collectors are interested in toys that fall into two categories.

Toys From Long Ago (Antiques)	*More Recent Toys*
Antiques must be at least one hundred years old. An antique toy in top condition can often be sold for thousands of dollars.	These toys cost less than top-quality antiques. They may remind older collectors of their childhood. Kids often collect them too.

All collectors, young or old, look for toys that are in excellent, or mint, condition. The most valuable toys are those that have never been played with.

Are you thinking of putting a new toy away and selling it to earn money later on? Then make sure to leave it in its box before you hide it safely away. Of course, you'll need some good luck too. There's no way of telling which toys are going to be "hot" items in the future!